Beyond Ideas of Right & Wrong

Words by Melissa Foks

Illustrations & design by Lucy Daniels
of www.dippyegg.net

This book is dedicated to
Camilla and Petronella...
and to sisters everywhere... and to anyone
anywhere in any kind of relationship with any
other person

Once upon a time there were two sisters who loved each other (because sisters always do really) but it certainly didn't seem that way.

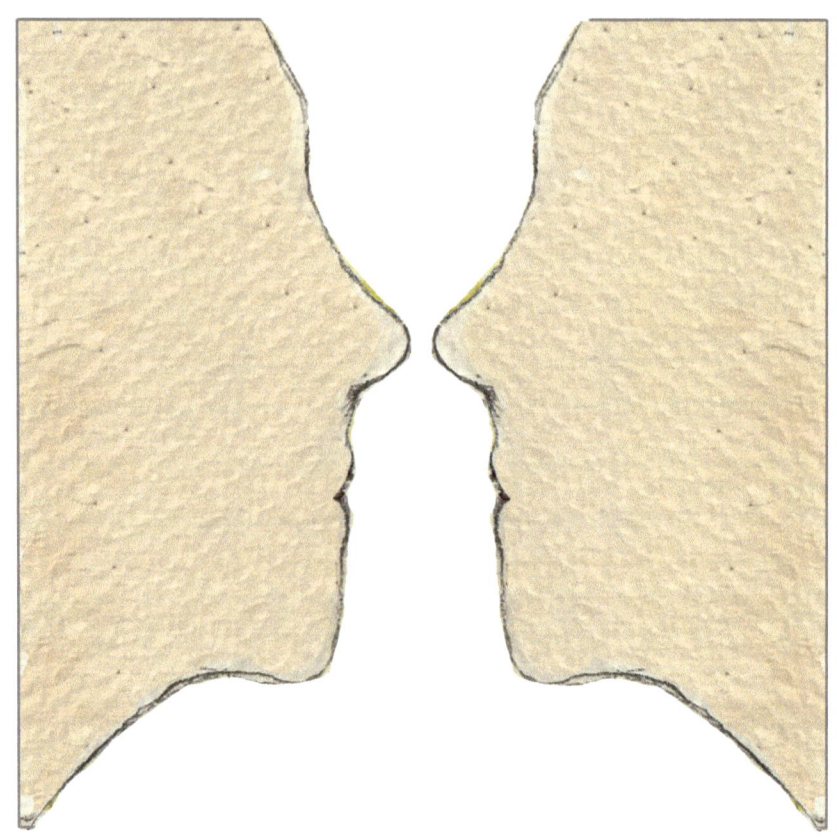

And the problem was this...

To one of the sisters it was two faces,
looking at each other.
'These people need a cup of tea'
she said, and hurried off to put the kettle on.

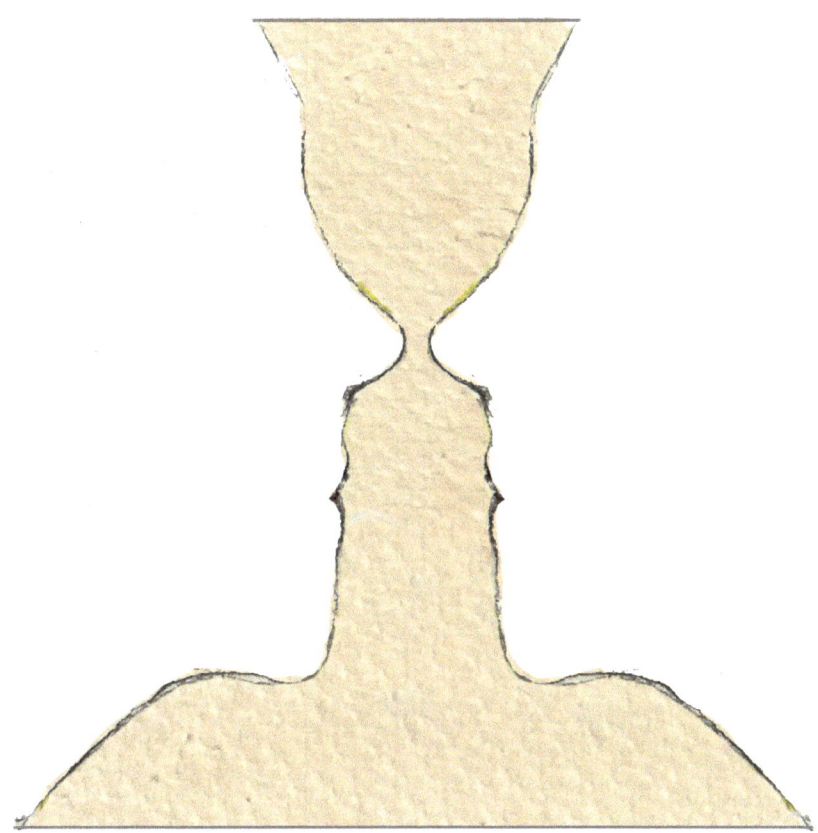

To the other sister it was a candlestick.
'We need some light here' she said,
and hurried off to fetch a candle.

"What the #%@&* are you doing?"
Shouted the first sister angrily.
"These people need a cup of tea.
I've put the kettle on and warmed
the pot, you just get the cups.
Make it snappy"

"People? What people?
Are you completely mad?
Leave me alone, I'm fetching a candle
to put in the candlestick...and a box
of matches"

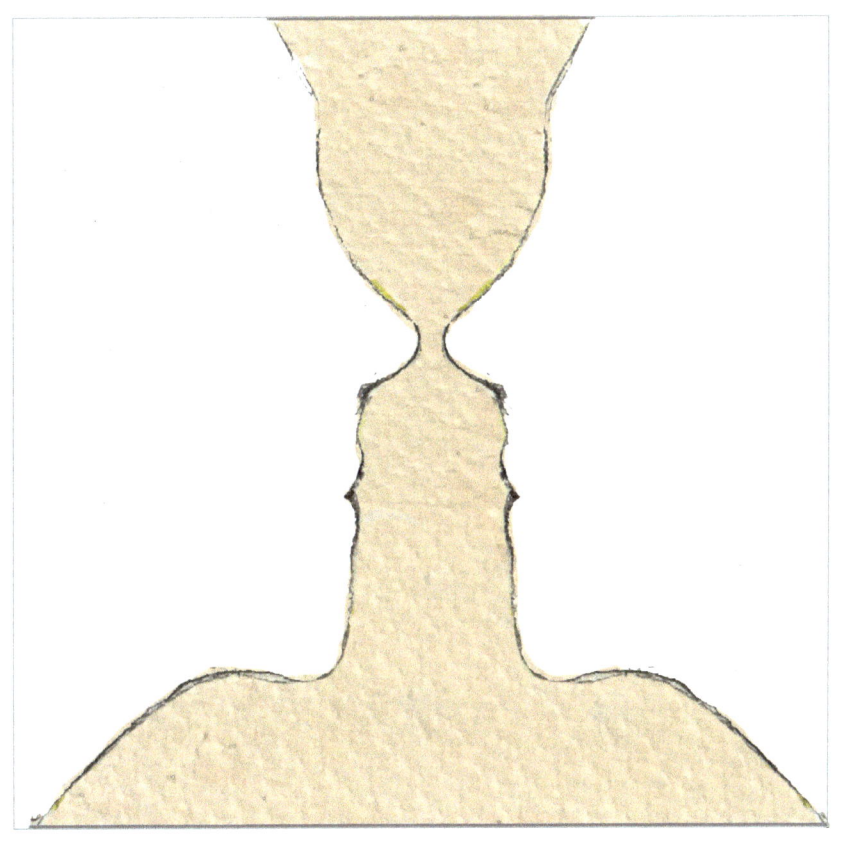

"People"
"Candlestick"
"People"
"Candlestick"

"People"

"Candlestick"

And so it went on, year after year…

Decade
after decade...

Until one day, their elderly mother became very ill.

Sitting at her bedside, the first sister asked
their Mother, "why do you pretend to her that you
see a candlestick, when you tell me that
you see two faces?"

Mother, "why do you
o faces, when
ck?"

"Well, I love you both very much; more than I can say. And the truth is that neither of you has ever been right. Nor wrong. Without the faces, can there be a candlestick? Without the candlestick can there be any faces?

Both are always here, and belong together. So perhaps what you see depends on how you look?"

In that moment, although it seemed like nothing
had really happened, *everything* had changed.
The sisters suddenly understood the words
"There's nothing right nor wrong, but thinking makes it so".
They came to understand how one another saw things,
and they all lived happily ever after...

THE END